# Simple Sabotage Field Manual

## Office of Strategic Services

OSS REPRODUCTION BRANCH
SIMPLE SABOTAGE FIELD MANUAL
Strategic Services
(Provisional)
STRATEGIC SERVICES FIELD MANUAL No. 3

Office of Strategic Services

Washington, D. C.

17 January 1944

This Simple Sabotage Field Manual Strategic Services (Provisional) is published for the information and guidance of all concerned and will be used as the basic doctrine for Strategic Services training for this subject.

The contents of this Manual should be carefully controlled and should not be allowed to come into unauthorized hands.

The instructions may be placed in separate pamphlets or leaflets according to categories of operations but should be distributed with care and not broadly. They should be used as a basis of radio broadcasts only for local and special cases and as directed by the theater commander.

AR 380-5, pertaining to handling of secret documents, will be complied with in the handling of this Manual.

William J. Donovan

# 1. **Office of Strategic Services**

The Office of Strategic Services (OSS) was the intelligence agency of the United States during World War II. The OSS was formed as an agency of the Joint Chiefs of Staff (JCS) to coordinate espionage activities behind enemy lines for all branches of the United States Armed Forces. Other OSS functions included the use of propaganda, subversion, and post-war planning.

The OSS was dissolved a month after the end of the war. Intelligence tasks were shortly later resumed and carried over by its successors the Department of State's Bureau of Intelligence and Research (INR), and the independent Central Intelligence Agency (CIA).

On December 14, 2016, the organization was collectively honored with a Congressional Gold Medal.

Origin

Prior to the formation of the OSS, the various departments of the executive branch, including the State, Treasury, Navy, and War Departments conducted American intelligence activities on an ad hoc basis, with no overall direction, coordination, or control. The US Army and US Navy had separate code-breaking departments: Signal Intelligence Service and OP-20-G. (A previous code-breaking operation of the State Department, the MI-8, run by Herbert Yardley, had been shut down in 1929 by Secretary of State Henry Stimson, deeming it an inappropriate function for the diplomatic arm, because "gentlemen don't read each other's mail.") The FBI was responsible for domestic security and anti-espionage operations.

President Franklin D. Roosevelt was concerned about American intelligence deficiencies. On the suggestion of William Stephenson, the senior British intelligence officer in the western hemisphere, Roosevelt requested that William J. Donovan draft a plan for an intelligence service based on the British Secret Intelligence Service (MI6) and Special Operations Executive (SOE). Donovan envisioned a single agency responsible for foreign intelligence and special operations involving commandos, disinformation, partisan and guerrilla activities. After submitting his work, "Memorandum of Establishment of Service of Strategic Information", he was appointed "coordinator of information" on July 11, 1941, heading the new organization known as the office of the Coordinator of Information (COI).

William J. Donovan

Thereafter the organization was developed with British assistance; Donovan had responsibilities but no actual powers and the existing US agencies were skeptical if not hostile. Until some months after Pearl Harbor, the bulk of OSS intelligence came from the UK. British Security Co-ordination (BSC) trained the first OSS agents in Canada, until training stations were set up in the US with guidance from BSC instructors, who also provided information on how the SOE was arranged and managed. The British immediately made available their short-wave broadcasting capabilities to Europe, Africa, and the Far East and provided equipment for agents until American production was established.

The Office of Strategic Services was established by a Presidential military order issued by President Roosevelt on June 13, 1942, to collect and analyze strategic information required by the Joint Chiefs of Staff and to conduct special operations not assigned to other agencies. During the war, the OSS supplied policymakers with facts and estimates, but the OSS never had jurisdiction over all foreign intelligence activities. The FBI was left responsible for intelligence work in Latin America, and the Army and Navy continued to develop and rely on their own sources of intelligence.

Activities

General William J. Donovan reviews Operational Group members in Bethesda, Maryland prior to their departure for China in 1945.

OSS missions and bases in East Asia

OSS proved especially useful in providing a worldwide overview of the German war effort, its strengths and weaknesses. In direct operations it was successful in supporting Operation Torch in French North Africa in 1942, where it identified pro-Allied potential supporters and located landing sites. OSS operations in neutral countries, especially Stockholm, Sweden, provided in-depth information on German advanced technology. The Madrid station set up agent networks in France that supported the Allied invasion of southern France in 1944. Most famous were the operations in Switzerland run by Allen Dulles that provided extensive information on German strength, air defenses, submarine production, and the V-1 and V-2 weapons. It revealed some of the secret German efforts in chemical and biological warfare. Switzerland's station also supported resistance fighters in France, Austria and Italy, and helped with the surrender of German forces in Italy in 1945.

For the duration of World War II, the Office of Strategic Services was conducting multiple activities and missions, including collecting intelligence by spying, performing acts of sabotage, waging propaganda war, organizing and coordinating anti-Nazi resistance groups in Europe, and providing military training for anti-Japanese guerrilla movements in Asia, among other things. At the height of its influence during World War II, the OSS employed almost 24,000 people.

From 1943–1945, the OSS played a major role in training Kuomintang troops in China and Burma, and recruited

Kachin and other indigenous irregular forces for sabotage as well as guides for Allied forces in Burma fighting the Japanese Army. Among other activities, the OSS helped arm, train, and supply resistance movements in areas occupied by the Axis powers during World War II, including Mao Zedong's Red Army in China (known as the Dixie Mission) and the Viet Minh in French Indochina. OSS officer Archimedes Patti played a central role in OSS operations in French Indochina and met frequently with Ho Chi Minh in 1945.

One of the greatest accomplishments of the OSS during World War II was its penetration of Nazi Germany by OSS operatives. The OSS was responsible for training German and Austrian individuals for missions inside Germany. Some of these agents included exiled communists and Socialist party members, labor activists, anti-Nazi prisoners-of-war, and German and Jewish refugees. The OSS also recruited and ran one of the war's most important spies, the German diplomat Fritz Kolbe.

From 1943 the OSS was in contact with the Austrian resistance group around Kaplan Heinrich Maier. As a result, plans and production facilities for V-2 rockets, Tiger tanks and aircraft (Messerschmitt Bf 109, Messerschmitt Me 163 Komet, etc.) were passed on to Allied general staffs in order to enable Allied bombers to get accurate air strikes. The Maier group informed very early about the mass murder of Jews through its contacts with the Semperit factory near

Auschwitz. The group was gradually dismantled by the German authorities because of a double agent who worked for both the OSS and the Gestapo. This uncovered a transfer of money from the Americans to Vienna via Istanbul and Budapest, and most of the members were executed after a People's Court hearing.

OSS 1st Lieutenant George Musulin behind enemy lines in German-occupied Serbia, as a Chetnik, during his first mission in November 1943. His second mission was Operation Halyard.

In 1943, the Office of Strategic Services set up operations in Istanbul. Turkey, as a neutral country during the Second World War, was a place where both the Axis and Allied powers had spy networks. The railroads connecting central Asia with Europe, as well as Turkey's close proximity to the Balkan states, placed it at a crossroads of intelligence gathering. The goal of the OSS Istanbul operation called Project Net-1 was to infiltrate and extenuate subversive action in the old Ottoman and Austro-Hungarian Empires.

The head of operations at OSS Istanbul was a banker from Chicago named Lanning "Packy" Macfarland, who maintained a cover story as a banker for the American lend-lease program.Macfarland hired Alfred Schwarz, a Czechoslovakian engineer and businessman who came to be known as "Dogwood" and ended up establishing the

Dogwood information chain. Dogwood in turn hired a personal assistant named Walter Arndt and established himself as an employee of the Istanbul Western Electrik Kompani. Through Schwartz and Arndt the OSS was able to infiltrate anti-fascist groups in Austria, Hungary, and Germany. Schwartz was able to convince Romanian, Bulgarian, Hungarian, and Swiss diplomatic couriers to smuggle American intelligence information into these territories and establish contact with elements antagonistic to the Nazis and their collaborators. Couriers and agents memorized information and produced analytical reports; when they were not able to memorize effectively they recorded information on microfilm and hid it in their shoes or hollowed pencils.Through this process information about the Nazi regime made its way to Macfarland and the OSS in Istanbul and eventually to Washington.

While the OSS "Dogwood-chain" produced a lot of information, its reliability was increasingly questioned by British intelligence. By May 1944, through collaboration between the OSS, British intelligence, Cairo, and Washington, the entire Dogwood-chain was found to be unreliable and dangerous. Planting phony information into the OSS was intended to misdirect the resources of the Allies. Schwartz's Dogwood-chain, which was the largest American intelligence gathering tool in occupied territory, was shortly thereafter shut down.

The OSS purchased Soviet code and cipher material (or Finnish information on them) from émigré Finnish army officers in late 1944. Secretary of State Edward Stettinius, Jr., protested that this violated an agreement President Roosevelt made with the Soviet Union not to interfere with Soviet cipher traffic from the United States. General Donovan might have copied the papers before returning them the following January, but there is no record of Arlington Hall receiving them, and CIA and NSA archives have no surviving copies. This codebook was in fact used as part of the Venona decryption effort, which helped uncover large-scale Soviet espionage in North America.

RYPE was the codename of the airborne unit who was dropped in the Norwegian mountains of Snåsa on March 24, 1945 to carry out sabotage actions behind enemy lines. From the base at the Gjefsjøen mountain farm, the group conducted successful railroad sabotages, with the intention of preventing the withdrawal of German forces from northern Norway. Operasjon Rype was the only U.S. operation on German-occupied Norwegian soil during WW2. The group consisted mainly of Norwegian Americans recruited from the 99th Infantry Battalion. Operasjon Rype was led by William Colby.

The OSS sent four teams of two under Captain Stephen Vinciguerra (codename Algonquin, teams Alsace, Poissy, S&S and Student), with Operation Varsity in March 1945 to infiltrate and report from behind enemy lines, but none succeeded. Team S&S had two agents in Wehrmacht uniforms and a captured Kübelwagon; to report by radio. But the Kübelwagon was put out of action while in the glider; three tires and the long-range radio were shot up (German gunners were told to attack the gliders not the tow planes).


Weapons and gadgets


OSS T13 Beano Grenade and compass hidden in a button, CIA Museum

The OSS espionage and sabotage operations produced a steady demand for highly specialized equipment. General Donovan invited experts, organized workshops, and funded labs that later formed the core of the Research & Development Branch. Boston chemist Stanley P. Lovell became its first head, and Donovan humorously called him his "Professor Moriarty". 101 Throughout the war years, the OSS Research & Development successfully adapted Allied weapons and espionage equipment, and produced its own line of novel spy tools and gadgets, including silenced pistols, lightweight sub-machine guns, "Beano" grenades that exploded upon impact, explosives disguised as lumps of coal ("Black Joe") or bags of Chinese flour ("Aunt Jemima"), acetone time delay fuses for limpet mines, compasses hidden in uniform buttons, playing cards that concealed maps, a 16mm Kodak camera in the shape of a matchbox, tasteless poison tablets ("K" and "L" pills), and cigarettes laced with tetrahydrocannabinol acetate (an extract of Indian hemp) to induce uncontrollable chattiness.

The OSS also developed innovative communication equipment such as wiretap gadgets, electronic beacons for locating agents, and the "Joan-Eleanor" portable radio system that made it possible for operatives on the ground to establish secure contact with a plane that was preparing to land or drop cargo. The OSS Research & Development also printed fake German and Japanese-issued identification cards, and various passes, ration cards, and counterfeit money.

On August 28, 1943, Stanley Lovell was asked to make a presentation in front of a hostile Joint Chiefs of Staff, who were skeptical of OSS plans beyond collecting military intelligence and were ready to split the OSS between the Army and the Navy.:5–7 While explaining the purpose and mission of his department and introducing various gadgets and tools, he reportedly casually dropped into a waste basket a Hedy, a panic-inducing explosive device in the shape of a firecracker, which shortly produced a loud shrieking sound followed by a deafening boom. The presentation was interrupted and did not resume since everyone in the room fled. In reality, the Hedy, jokingly named after Hollywood movie star Hedy Lamarr for her ability to distract men, later saved the lives of some trapped OSS operatives.:184–185

Not all projects worked. Some ideas were odd, such as a failed attempt to use insects to spread anthrax in Spain.:150–151 Stanley Lovell was later quoted saying, "It was my policy to consider any method whatever that might aid the war, however unorthodox or untried".

In 1939, a young physician named Christian J. Lambertsen developed an oxygen rebreather set (the Lambertsen Amphibious Respiratory Unit) and demonstrated it to the OSS—after already being rejected by the U.S. Navy—in a pool at the Shoreham Hotel in Washington D.C., in 1942. The OSS not only bought into the concept, they hired Lambertsen to lead the program and build up the dive element for the organization. His responsibilities included training and developing methods of combining self-contained diving and swimmer delivery including the Lambertsen Amphibious Respiratory Unit for the OSS "Operational Swimmer Group". Growing involvement of the OSS with coastal infiltration and water-based sabotage eventually led to creation of the OSS Maritime Unit.

Facilities

At Camp X, near Whitby, Ontario, an "assassination and elimination" training program was operated by the British Special Operations Executive, assigning exceptional masters in the art of knife-wielding combat, such as William E. Fairbairn and Eric A. Sykes, to instruct trainees. Many members of the Office of Strategic Services also were trained there. It was dubbed "the school of mayhem and murder" by George Hunter White who trained at the facility in the 1950s.

From these incipient beginnings, the Office of Strategic Services opened camps in the United States, and finally abroad. Prince William Forest Park (then known as Chopawamsic Recreational Demonstration Area) was the site of an OSS training camp that operated from 1942 to 1945. Area "C", consisting of approximately 6,000 acres (24 km2), was used extensively for communications training, whereas Area "A" was used for training some of the OGs (Operational Groups). Catoctin Mountain Park, now the location of Camp David, was the site of OSS training Area "B" where the first Special Operations, or SO, were trained. Special Operations was modeled after Great Britain's Special Operations Executive, which included parachute, sabotage, self-defense, weapons, and leadership training to support guerrilla or partisan resistance. Considered most mysterious of all was the "cloak and dagger" Secret Intelligence, or SI branch. Secret Intelligence employed "country estates as schools for introducing recruits into the murky world of espionage. Thus, it established Training Areas E and RTU-11 ("the Farm") in spacious manor houses with surrounding horse farms." Morale Operations training included psychological warfare and propaganda. The Congressional Country Club (Area F) in Bethesda, Maryland, was the primary OSS training facility. The Facilities of the Catalina Island Marine Institute at Toyon Bay on Santa Catalina Island, Calif., are composed (in part) of a former OSS survival training camp. The National Park Service commissioned a study of OSS National Park training facilities by Professor John Chambers of Rutgers University.

The main OSS training camps abroad were located initially in Great Britain, French Algeria, and Egypt; later as the Allies advanced, a school was established in southern Italy. In the Far East, OSS training facilities were established in India, Ceylon, and then China. The London branch of the OSS, its first overseas facility, was at 70 Grosvenor Street, W1. In addition to training local agents, the overseas OSS schools also provided advanced training and field exercises for graduates of the training camps in the United States and for Americans who enlisted in the OSS in the war zones. The most famous of the latter was Virginia Hall in France.

The OSS's Mediterranean training center in Cairo, Egypt, known to many as the Spy School, was a lavish palace belonging to King Farouk's brother-in-law, called Ras el Kanayas. It was modeled after the SOE's training facility STS 102 in Haifa, Palestine. Americans whose heritage stemmed from Italy, Yugoslavia, and Greece were trained at the "Spy School" and also sent for parachute, weapons, and commando training, and Morse code and encryption lessons at STS 102. After completion of their spy training, these agents were sent back on missions to the Balkans and Italy where their accents would not pose a problem for their assimilation.

Personnel

The names of all 13,000 OSS personnel and documents of their OSS service, previously a closely guarded secret, were released by the US National Archives on August 14, 2008. Among the 24,000 names were those of Sterling Hayden, Carl C. Cable, Julia Child, Ralph Bunche, Arthur Goldberg, Saul K. Padover, Arthur Schlesinger, Jr., Bruce Sundlun, William Colby, René Joyeuse, and John Ford. The 750,000 pages in the 35,000 personnel files include applications of people who were not recruited or hired, as well as the service records of those who served.

OSS soldiers were primarily inducted from the United States Armed Forces. Other members included foreign nationals including displaced individuals from the former czarist Russia, an example being Prince Serge Obolensky.

Donovan sought independent thinkers, and in order to bring together those many intelligent, quick-witted individuals who could think out-of-the box, he chose them from all walks of life, backgrounds, without distinction to culture or religion. Donovan was quoted as saying, "I'd rather have a young lieutenant with enough guts to disobey a direct order than a colonel too regimented to think for himself." In a matter of a few short months, he formed an organization which equalled and then rivalled Great Britain's Secret Intelligence Service and its Special Operations Executive. Donovan, inspired by Britain's SOE, assembled an outstanding group of clinical psychologists to carry out evaluations of potential OSS candidates at a variety of sites, primary among these was Station S in Northern Virginia near where Dulles International Airport now stands. Recent research from remaining records from the OSS Station S program describes how those characteristics (independent thought, effective intelligence, interpersonal skills) were found among OSS candidates

Major league baseball player Moe Berg of the Boston Red Sox was an OSS agent

One such agent was Ivy League polyglot and Jewish American baseball catcher Moe Berg, who played 15 seasons in the major leagues. As a Secret Intelligence agent, he was dispatched to seek information on German physicist Werner Heisenberg and his knowledge on the atomic bomb. One of the most highly decorated and flamboyant OSS soldiers was US Marine Colonel Peter Ortiz. Enlisting early in the war, as a French Foreign Legionnaire, he went on to join the OSS and to be the most highly decorated US Marine in the OSS during World War II.

Col. Peter Ortiz, USMC

Julia Child, who later authored cookbooks, worked directly under Donovan.

René Joyeuse M.D., MS, FACS was a Swiss, French and American soldier, physician and researcher, who distinguished himself as an agent of Allied intelligence in German-occupied France during World War II. He received the US Army Distinguished Service Cross for his actions with the OSS, after the war he became a Physician, Researcher and was a co-founder of The American Trauma Society.

"Jumping Joe" Savoldi (code name Sampson) was recruited by the OSS in 1942 because of his hand-to-hand combat and language skills as well as his deep knowledge of the Italian geography and Benito Mussolini's compound. He was assigned to the Special Operations branch and took part in missions in North Africa, Italy, and France during 1943–1945.

OSS created this false ID for Joe Savoldi - posing as Giuseppe De Leo while infiltrating the black market in Naples

One of the forefathers of today's commandos was Navy Lieutenant Jack Taylor. He was sequestered by the OSS early in the war and had a long career behind enemy lines.

Taro and Mitsu Yashima, both Japanese political dissidents who were imprisoned in Japan for protesting its militarist regime, worked for the OSS in psychological warfare against the Japanese Empire.

## Nisei linguists

In late 1943, a representative from OSS visited the 442nd Infantry Regiment looking to recruit volunteers willing to undertake "extremely hazardous assignment." All selected were Nisei. The recruits were assigned to OSS Detachments 101 and 202, in the China-Burma-India Theater. "Once deployed, they were to interrogate prisoners, translate documents, monitor radio communications, and conduct covert operations... Detachment 101 and 102's clandestine operations were extremely successful."

## Dissolution into other agencies

On September 20, 1945, President Truman signed Executive Order 9621, terminating the OSS. The State Department took over the Research and Analysis Branch; it became the Bureau of Intelligence and Research, The War Department took over the Secret Intelligence (SI) and Counter-Espionage (X-2) Branches, which were then housed in the new Strategic Services Unit (SSU). Brigadier General John Magruder (formerly Donovan's Deputy Director for Intelligence in OSS) became the new SSU director. He oversaw the liquidation of the OSS and managed the institutional preservation of its clandestine intelligence capability.

In January 1946, President Truman created the Central Intelligence Group (CIG), which was the direct precursor to the CIA. SSU assets, which now constituted a streamlined "nucleus" of clandestine intelligence, were transferred to the CIG in mid-1946 and reconstituted as the Office of Special Operations (OSO). The National Security Act of 1947 established the Central Intelligence Agency, which then took up some OSS functions. The direct descendant of the paramilitary component of the OSS is the CIA Special Activities Division.

Today, the joint-branch United States Special Operations Command, founded in 1987, uses the same spearhead design on its insignia, as homage to its indirect lineage. The Defense Intelligence Agency currently manages the OSS' mandate to provide strategic military intelligence to the Joint Chiefs of Staff and the Secretary of Defense and to coordinate human espionage activities across the United States Armed Forces (through the Defense Clandestine Service) and was awarded status as an OSS Heritage organization by the OSS Society.

From Wikipedia, the free encyclopedia

# 2. INTRODUCTION

The purpose of this paper is to characterize simple sabotage, to outline its possible effects, and to present suggestions for inciting and executing it.

Sabotage varies from highly technical *coup de main* acts that require detailed planning and the use of specially-trained operatives, to innumerable simple acts which the ordinary individual citizen-saboteur can perform. This paper is primarily concerned with the latter type. Simple sabotage does not require specially prepared tools or equipment; it is executed by an ordinary citizen who may or may not act individually and without the necessity for active connection with an organized group; and it is carried out in such a way as to involve a minimum danger of injury, detection, and reprisal.

Where destruction is involved, the weapons of the citizen-saboteur are salt, nails, candles, pebbles, thread, or any other materials he might normally be expected to possess as a householder or as a worker in his particular occupation. His arsenal is the kitchen shelf, the trash pile, his own usual kit of tools and supplies. The targets of his sabotage are usually objects to which he has normal and inconspicuous access in everyday life.

A second type of simple sabotage requires no destructive tools whatsoever and produces physical damage, if any, by highly indirect means. It is based on universal opportunities to make faulty decisions, to adopt a noncooperative attitude, and to induce others to follow suit. Making a faulty decision may be simply a matter of placing tools in one spot instead of another. A non-cooperative attitude may involve nothing more than creating an unpleasant situation among one's fellow workers, engaging in bickerings, or displaying surliness and stupidity.

This type of activity, sometimes referred to as the "human element," is frequently responsible for accidents, delays, and general obstruction even under normal conditions. The potential saboteur should discover what types of faulty decisions and the operations are *normally* found in this kind of work and should then devise his sabotage so as to enlarge that "margin for error."

# 3. POSSIBLE EFFECTS

Acts of simple sabotage are occurring throughout Europe. An effort should be made to add to their efficiency, lessen their detectability, and increase their number. Acts of simple sabotage, multiplied by thousands of citizen-saboteurs, can be an effective weapon against the enemy. Slashing tires, draining fuel tanks, starting fires, starting arguments, acting stupidly, short-circuiting electric systems, abrading machine parts will waste materials, manpower, and time. Occurring on a wide scale, simple sabotage will be a constant and tangible drag on the war effort of the enemy.

Simple sabotage may also have secondary results of more or less value. Widespread practice of simple sabotage will harass and demoralize enemy administrators and police. Further, success may embolden the citizen-saboteur eventually to find colleagues who can assist him in sabotage of greater dimensions. Finally, the very practice of simple sabotage by natives in enemy or occupied territory may make these individuals identify themselves actively with the United Nations war effort, and encourage them to assist openly in periods of Allied invasion and occupation.

# 4. MOTIVATING THE SABOTEUR

To incite the citizen to the active practice of simple sabotage and to keep him practicing that sabotage over sustained periods is a special problem.

Simple sabotage is often an act which the citizen performs according to his own initiative and inclination. Acts of destruction do not bring him any personal gain and may be completely foreign to his habitually conservationist attitude toward materials and tools. Purposeful stupidity is contrary to human nature. He frequently needs pressure, stimulation or assurance, and information and suggestions regarding feasible methods of simple sabotage.

(1) *Personal Motives*

(a) The ordinary citizen very probably has no immediate personal motive for committing simple sabotage. Instead, he must be made to anticipate indirect personal gain, such as might come with enemy evacuation or destruction of the ruling government group. Gains should be stated as specifically as possible for the area addressed: simple sabotage will hasten the day when Commissioner X and his deputies Y and Z will be thrown out, when particularly obnoxious decrees and restrictions will be abolished, when food will arrive, and so on. Abstract verbalizations about personal liberty, freedom of the press, and so on, will not be convincing in most parts of the world. In many areas they will not even be comprehensible.

(b) Since the effect of his own acts is limited, the saboteur may become discouraged unless he feels that he is a member of a large, though unseen, group of saboteurs operating against the enemy or the government of his own country and elsewhere. This can be conveyed indirectly: suggestions which he reads and hears can include observations that a particular technique has been successful in this or that district. Even if the technique is not applicable to his surroundings, another's success will encourage him to attempt similar acts. It also can be conveyed directly: statements praising the effectiveness of simple sabotage can be contrived which will be published by white radio, freedom stations, and the subversive press. Estimates of the proportion of the population engaged in sabotage can be disseminated. Instances of successful sabotage already are being broadcast by white radio and freedom stations, and this should be continued and expanded where compatible with security.

(c) More important than (a) or (b) would be to create a situation in which the citizen-saboteur acquires a sense of responsibility and begins to educate others in simple sabotage.

(2) *Encouraging Destructiveness*

It should be pointed out to the saboteur where the circumstances are suitable, that he is acting in self-defense against the enemy, or retaliating against the enemy for other acts of destruction. A reasonable amount of humor in the presentation of suggestions for simple sabotage will relax tensions of fear.

(a) The saboteur may have to reverse his thinking, and he should be told this in so many words. Where he formerly thought of keeping his tools sharp, he should now let them grow dull; surfaces that formerly were lubricated now should be sanded; normally diligent, he should now be lazy and careless; and so on. Once he is encouraged to think backwards about himself and the objects of his everyday life, the saboteur will see many opportunities in his immediate environment which cannot possibly be seen from a distance. A state of mind should be encouraged that anything can be sabotaged.

(b) Among the potential citizen-saboteurs who are to engage in physical destruction, two extreme types may be distinguished. On the one hand, there is the man who is not technically trained and employed. This man needs specific suggestions as to what he can and should destroy as well as details regarding the tools by means of which destruction is accomplished.

(c) At the other extreme is the man who is a technician, such as a lathe operator or an automobile mechanic. Presumably this man would be able to devise methods of simple sabotage which would be appropriate to his own facilities. However, this man needs to be stimulated to re-orient his thinking in the direction of destruction. Specific examples, which need not be from his own field, should accomplish this.

(d) Various media may be used to disseminate suggestions and information regarding simple sabotage. Among the media which may be used, as the immediate situation dictates, are: freedom stations or radio false (unreadable) broadcasts or leaflets may be directed toward specific geographic or occupational areas, or they may be general in scope. Finally, agents may be trained in the art of simple sabotage, in anticipation of a time when they may be able to communicate this information directly.

(3) *Safety Measures*

(a) The amount of activity carried on by the saboteur will be governed not only by the number of opportunities he sees, but also by the amount of danger he feels. Bad news travels fast, and simple sabotage will be discouraged if too many simple saboteurs are arrested.

(b) It should not be difficult to prepare leaflets and other media for the saboteur about the choice of weapons, time, and targets which will insure the saboteur against detection and retaliation. Among such suggestions might be the following:

(1) Use materials which appear to be innocent. A knife or a nail file can be carried normally on your person; either is a

multi-purpose instrument for creating damage. Matches, pebbles, hair, salt, nails, and dozens of other destructive agents can be carried or kept in your living quarters without exciting any suspicion whatever. If you are a worker in a particular trade or industry you can easily carry and keep such things as wrenches, hammers, emery paper, and the like.

(2) Try to commit acts for which large numbers of people could be responsible. For instance, if you blow out the wiring in a factory at a central fire box, almost anyone could have done it. On-the-street sabotage after dark, such as you might be able to carry out against a military car or truck, is another example of an act for which it would be impossible to blame you.

(3) Do not be afraid to commit acts for which you might be blamed directly, so long as you do so rarely, and as long as you have a plausible excuse: you dropped your wrench across an electric circuit because an air raid had kept you up the night before and you were half-dozing at work. Always be profuse in your apologies. Frequently you can "get away" with such acts under the cover of pretending stupidity, ignorance, over-caution, fear of being suspected of sabotage, or weakness and dullness due to undernourishment.

(4) After you have committed an act of easy sabotage, resist any temptation to wait around and see what happens. Loiterers arouse suspicion. Of course, there are circumstances when it would be suspicious for you to leave. If you commit sabotage on your job, you should naturally stay at your work.

# 5. TOOLS, TARGETS, AND TIMING

The citizen-saboteur cannot be closely controlled. Nor is it reasonable to expect that simple sabotage can be precisely concentrated on specific types of target according to the requirements of a concrete military situation. Attempts to control simple sabotage according to developing military factors, moreover, might provide the enemy with intelligence of more or less value in anticipating the date and area of notably intensified or notably slackened military activity.

Sabotage suggestions, of course, should be adapted to fit the area where they are to be practiced. Target priorities for general types of situations likewise can be specified, for emphasis at the proper time by the underground press, freedom stations, and cooperating propaganda.

(1) *Under General Conditions*

(a) Simple sabotage is more than malicious mischief, and it should always consist of acts whose results will be detrimental to the materials and manpower of the enemy.

(b) The saboteur should be ingenious in using his every-day equipment. All sorts of weapons will present themselves if he looks at his surroundings in a different light. For example, emery dust—a at first may seen unobtainable but if the saboteur were to pulverize an emery knife sharpener or emery wheel with a hammer, he would find himself with a plentiful supply.

(c) The saboteur should never attack targets beyond his capacity or the capacity of his instruments. An inexperienced person should not, for example, attempt to use explosives, but should confine himself to the use of matches or other familiar weapons.

(d) The saboteur should try to damage only objects and materials known to be in use by the enemy or to be destined for early use by the enemy. It will be safe for him to assume that almost any product of heavy industry is destined for enemy use, and that the most efficient fuels and lubricants also are destined for enemy use. Without special knowledge, however, it would be undesirable for him to attempt destruction of food crops or food products.

(e) Although the citizen-saboteur may rarely have access to military objects, he should give these preference above all others.

(2) *Prior to a Military Offensive*

During periods which are quiescent in a military sense, such emphasis as can be given to simple sabotage might well center on industrial production, to lessen the flow of materials and equipment to the enemy. Slashing a rubber tire on an Army truck may be an act of value; spoiling a batch of rubber in the production plant is an act of still more value.

(3) *During a Military Offensive*

(a) Most significant sabotage for an area which is, or is soon destined to be, a theater of combat operations is that whose effects will be direct and immediate. Even if the effects are relatively minor and localized, this type of sabotage is to be preferred to activities whose effects, while widespread, are indirect and delayed.

(1) The saboteur should be encouraged to attack transportation facilities of all kinds.

Among such facilities are roads, railroads, auto mobiles, trucks, motor-cycles, bicycles, trains, and trams.

(2) Any communications facilities which can be used by the authorities to transmit instructions or morale material should be the objects of simple sabotage. These include telephone, telegraph and power systems, radio, newspapers, placards, and public notices.

(3) Critical materials, valuable in themselves or necessary to the efficient functioning of transportation and

communication, also should become targets for the citizen-saboteur. These may include oil, gasoline, tires, food, and water.

# 6. SPECIFIC SUGGESTIONS FOR SIMPLE SABOTAGE

It will not be possible to evaluate the desirability of simple sabotage in an area without having in mind rather specifically what individual acts and results are embraced by the definition of simple sabotage.

A listing of specific acts follows, classified according to types of target. This list is presented as a growing rather than a complete outline of the methods of simple sabotage. As new techniques are developed, or new fields explored, it will be elaborated and expanded.

(1) *Buildings*

Warehouses, barracks, offices, hotels, and factory buildings are outstanding targets for simple sabotage. They are extremely susceptible to damage, especially by fire; they offer opportunities to such untrained people as janitors, charwomen, and casual visitors; and, when damaged, they present a relatively large handicap to the enemy.

(a) *Fires* can be started wherever there is an accumulation of inflammable material. Warehouses are obviously the most promising targets but incendiary sabotage need not be confined to them alone.

(1) Whenever possible, arrange to have the fire start after you have gone away. Use a candle and paper, combination, setting it as close as possible to the inflammable material you want to burn: From a sheet of paper, tear a strip three or four centimeters wide and wrap it around the base of the candle two or three times. Twist more sheets of paper into loose ropes and place them around the base of the candle. When the candle flame reaches the encircling strip, it will be ignited and in turn will ignite the surrounding paper. The size, heat, and duration of the resulting flame will depend on how much paper you use and how much of it you can cramp in a small space.

(2) With a flame of this kind, do not attempt to ignite any but rather inflammable materials, such as cotton sacking. To

light more resistant materials, use a candle plus tightly rolled or twisted paper which has been soaked in gasoline. To create a briefer but even hotter flame, put celluloid such as you might find in an old comb, into a nest of plain or saturated paper which is to be fired by a candle.

(3) To make another type of simple fuse, soak one end of a piece of string in grease. Rub a generous pinch of gunpowder over the inch of string where greasy string meets clean string. Then ignite the clean end of the string. It will burn slowly without a flame (in much the same way that a cigarette burns) until it reaches the grease and gunpowder; it will then flare up suddenly. The grease-treated string will then burn with a flame. The same effect may be achieved by using matches instead of the grease and gunpowder. Run the string over the match heads, taking care that the string is not pressed or knotted. They too will produce a sudden flame. The advantage of this type of fuse is that string burns at a set speed. You can time your fire by the length and thickness of the string you chose.

(4) Use a fuse such as; the ones suggested above to start a fire in an office after hours. The destruction of records and other types of documents would be a serious handicap to the enemy.

(5) In basements where waste is kept, janitors should accumulate oily and greasy waste. Such waste sometimes ignites spontaneously, but it can easily be lit with a cigarette or match. If you are a janitor on night duty, you can be the first to report the fire, but don't report it too soon.

(6) A clean factory is not susceptible to fire, but a dirty one is. Workers should be careless with refuse and janitors should be inefficient in cleaning. If enough dirt and trash can be accumulated an otherwise fireproof building will become inflammable.

(7) Where illuminating gas is used in a room which is vacant at night, shut the windows tightly, turn on the gas, and leave a candle burning in the room, closing the door tightly behind you. After a time, the gas will explode, and a fire may or may not follow.

(b) *Water and miscellaneous*

(1) Ruin warehouse stock by setting the automatic sprinkler system to work. You can do this by tapping the sprinkler heads sharply with a hammer or by holding a match under them.

(2) Forget to provide paper in toilets; put tightly rolled paper, hair, and other obstructions in the W. C. Saturate a sponge with a thick starch or sugar solution. Squeeze it tightly into a ball, wrap it with string, and dry. Remove the string when fully dried. The sponge will be in the form of a tight hard ball. Flush down a

W. C. or otherwise introduce into a sewer line. The sponge will gradually expand to its normal size and plug the sewage system.

(3) Put a coin beneath a bulb in a public building during the daytime, so that fuses will blow out when lights are turned on at night. The fuses themselves may be rendered ineffective by putting a coin behind them or loading them with heavy wire. Then a short-circuit may either start a fire, damage transformers, or blow out a central fuse which will interrupt distribution of electricity to a large area.

(4) Jam paper, bits of wood, hairpins, and anything else that will fit, into the locks of all unguarded entrances to public buildings.

(2) *Industrial Production: Manufacturing*

(a) Tools

(1) Let cutting tools grow dull. They will be inefficient, will slow down production, and may damage the materials and parts you use them on.

(2) Leave saws slightly twisted when you are not using them. After a while, they will break when used.

(3) Using a very rapid stroke will wear out a file before its time. So will dragging a file in slow strokes under heavy pressure. Exert pressure on the backward stroke as well as the forward stroke.

(4) Clean files by knocking them against the vise or the workpiece; they are easily broken this way.

(5) Bits and drills will snap under heavy pressure.

(6) You can put a press punch out of order by putting in it more material than it is adjusted for—two blanks instead of one, for example.

(7) Power-driven tools like pneumatic drills, riveters, and so on, are never efficient when dirty. Lubrication points and electric contacts can easily be fouled by normal accumulations of dirt or the insertion of foreign matter.

(b) Oil and lubrication systems are not only vulnerable to easy sabotage, but are critical in every machine with moving parts. Sabotage of oil and lubrication will slow production or stop work entirely at strategic points in industrial processes.

(1) Put metal dust or filings, fine sand, ground glass, emery dust (get it by pounding up an emery knife sharpener) and similar hard, gritty substances directly into lubrication systems. They will scour smooth surfaces, ruining pistons, cylinder walls, shafts, and bearings. They will overheat and stop motors which will need overhauling, new parts, and extensive repairs. Such materials, if they are used, should be introduced into lubrication systems past any filters which otherwise would strain them out.

(2) You can cause wear on any machine by uncovering a filter system, poking a pencil or any other sharp object through the filter mesh, then covering it up again. Or, if you can dispose of it quickly, simply remove the filter.

(3) If you cannot get at the lubrication system or filter directly, you may be able to lessen the effectiveness of oil by diluting it in storage. In this case, almost any liquid will do which will thin the oil. A small amount of sulphuric acid, varnish, water-glass, or linseed oil will be especially effective.

(4) Using a thin oil where a heavy oil is prescribed will break down a machine or heat up a moving shaft so that it will "freeze" and stop.

(5) Put any clogging substance into lubrication systems or, if it will float, into stored oil. Twisted combings of human hair, pieces of string, dead insects, and many other common objects will be effective in stopping or hindering the flow of oil through feed lines and filters.

(6) Under some circumstances, you may be able to destroy oil outright rather than interfere with its effectiveness, by removing stop-plugs from lubricating systems or by puncturing the drums and cans in which it is stored.

(c) Cooling Systems (1.) A water cooling system can be put out of commission in a fairly short time, with considerable damage to an engine or motor, if you put into it several pinches of hard grain, such as rice or wheat. They will swell up and choke the circulation of water, and the cooling system will have to be torn down to remove the obstruction. Sawdust or hair may also be used to clog a water cooling system.

(2) If very cold water is quickly introduced into the cooling system of an overheated motor, contraction and considerable strain on the engine housing will result. If you can repeat the

treatment a few times, cracking and serious damage will result.

(3) You can ruin the effectiveness of an air cooling system by plugging dirt and waste into intake or exhaust valves. If a belt-run fan is used in the system, make a jagged cut at least half way through the belt; it will slip and finally part under strain and the motor will overheat.

(d) Gasoline and Oil Fuel Tanks and fueling engines usually are accessible and easy to open. They afford a very vulnerable target for simple sabotage activities. (1.) Put several pinches of sawdust or hard grain, such as rice or wheat, into the fuel tank of a gasoline engine. The particles will choke a feed line so that the engine will stop. Some time will be required to discover the source of the trouble. Although they will be hard to get, crumbs of natural rubber, such as you might find in old rubber bands and pencil erasers, are also effective.

(2) If you can accumulate sugar, put it in the fuel tank of a gasoline engine. As it burns together with the gasoline, it will turn into a sticky mess which will completely mire the engine and necessitate extensive cleaning and repair. Honey and molasses are as good as sugar. Try to use about 75–100 grams for each 10 gallons of gasoline.

(3) Other impurities which you can introduce into gasoline will cause rapid engine wear and eventual breakdown. Fine particles of pumice, sand, ground glass, and metal dust can easily be introduced into a gasoline tank. Be sure that the particles are very fine, so that they will be able to pass through the carburetor jet.

(4) Water, urine, wine, or any other simple liquid you can get in reasonably large quantities will dilute gasoline fuel to a point where no combustion will occur in the cylinder and the engine will not move. One pint to 20 gallons of gasoline is

sufficient. If salt water is used, it will cause corrosion and permanent motor damage.

(5) In the case of Diesel engines, put low flashpoint oil into the fuel tank; the engine will not move. If there already is proper oil in the tank when the wrong kind is added, the engine will only limp and sputter along.

(6) Fuel lines to gasoline and oil engines frequently pass over the exhaust pipe. When the machine is at rest, you can stab a small hole in the fuel line and plug the hole with wax. As the engine runs and the exhaust tube becomes hot, the wax will be melted; fuel will drip onto the exhaust and a blaze will start.

(7) If you have access to a room where gasoline is stored, remember that gas vapor accumulating in a closed room will explode after a time if you leave a candle burning in the room. A good deal of evaporation, however, must occur from the gasoline tins into the air of the room. If removal of the tops of the tins does not expose enough gasoline to the air to ensure copious evaporation, you can open lightly constructed tins further with a knife, ice pick or sharpened nail file. Or puncture a tiny hole in the tank which will permit gasoline to leak out on the floor. This will greatly increase the rate of evaporation. Before you light your candle, be sure that windows are closed and the room is as air-tight as you can make it. If you can see that windows in a neighboring room are opened wide, you have a chance of setting a large fire which will not only destroy the gasoline but anything else nearby; when the gasoline explodes, the doors of the storage room will be blown open, a draft to the neighboring windows will be created which will whip up a fine conflagration.

(e) Electric Motors Electric motors (including dynamos) are more restricted than the targets so far discussed. They cannot be sabotaged easily or without risk of injury by unskilled persons who may otherwise have good opportunities for destruction.

(1) Set the rheostat to a high point of resistance in all types of electric motors. They will overheat and catch fire.

(2) Adjust the overload relay to a very high value beyond the capacity of the motor. Then overload the motor to a point where it will overheat and break down.

(3) Remember that dust, dirt, and moisture are enemies of electrical equipment. Spill dust and dirt onto the points where the wires in electric motors connect with terminals, and onto insulating parts. Inefficient transmission of current and, in some cases, short circuits will result. Wet generator motors to produce short circuits.

(4) "Accidentally" bruise the insulation on wire, loosen nuts on connections, make faulty splices and faulty connections in wiring, to waste electric current and reduce the power of electric motors, the power output or cause short circuiting in direct-current motors: Loosen or remove commutator holding rings. Sprinkle carbon, graphite, or metal dust on commutators. Put a little grease or oil at the contact points of commutators. Where commutator bars are close together bridge the gaps between them with metal dust, or sawtooth their edges with a chisel so that the teeth on adjoining bars meet or nearly meet and current can pass from one to the other.

(6) Put a piece of finely grained emery paper half the size of a postage stamp in a place where it will wear away rotating brushes. The emery paper and the motor will be destroyed in the resulting fire.

(7) Sprinkle carbon, graphite or metal dust on slip-rings so that the current will leak or short circuits will occur. When a motor is idle, nick the slip-rings with a chisel.

(8) Cause motor stoppage or inefficiency by applying dust mixed with grease to the face of the armature so that it will not make proper contact.

(9) To overheat electric motors, mix sand with heavy grease and smear it between the stator and rotor, or wedge thin metal pieces between them. To prevent the efficient generation of current, put floor sweepings, oil, tar, or paint between them.

(10) In motors using three-phase current, deeply nick one of the lead-in wires with a knife or file when the machine is at rest, or replace one of the three fuses with a blown-out fuse. In the first case, the motor will stop after running awhile, and in the second, it will not start.

(f) Transformers

(1) Transformers of the oil-filled type can be put out of commission if you pour water, salt water, machine-tool coolant, or kerosene into the oil tank.

(2) In air-cooled transformers, block the ventilation by piling debris around the transformer.

(3) In all types of transformers, throw carbon, graphite or metal dust over the outside bushings and other exposed electrical parts.

(g) Turbines for the most part are heavily built, stoutly housed, and difficult of access. Their vulnerability to simple sabotage is very low.

(1) After inspecting or repairing a hydro turbine, fasten the cover insecurely so that it will blow off and flood the plant with water. A loose cover on a steam turbine will cause it to leak and slow down.

(2) In water turbines, insert a large piece of scrap iron in the head of the penstock, just beyond the screening, so that water will carry the damaging material down to the plant equipment.

(3) When the steam line to a turbine is opened for repair, put pieces of scrap iron into it, to be blasted into the turbine machinery when steam is up again.

(4) Create a leak in the line feeding oil to the turbine, so that oil will fall on the hot steam pipe and cause a fire.

(h) Boilers

(1) Reduce the efficiency of steam boilers any way you can. Put too much water in them to make them slow-starting, or keep the fire under them low to keep them inefficient. Let them dry and turn the fire up; they will crack and be ruined. An especially good trick is to keep putting limestone or water containing lime in the boiler; it will deposit lime on the bottom and sides. This deposit will provide very good insulation against heat; after enough of it has collected, the boiler will be completely worthless.

(3) *Production. Metals*

(a) Iron and Steel

(1) Keep blast furnaces in a condition where they must be frequently shut down for repair. In making fire-proof bricks for the inner lining of blast furnaces, put in an extra proportion of tar so that they will wear out quickly and necessitate constant re-lining.

(2) Make cores for casting so that they are filled with air bubbles and an imperfect cast results.

(3) See that the core in a mold is not properly supported, so that the core gives way or the casting is spoiled because of the incorrect position of the core.

(4) In tempering steel or iron, apply too much heat, so that the resulting bars and ingots are of poor quality.

(b) Other Metals

No suggestions available.

(4) *Production: Mining and Mineral Extraction*

(a) Coal

(1) A slight blow against your Davy oil lamp will extinguish it, and to light it again you will have to find a place where there is no fire damp. Take a long time looking for the place.

(2) Blacksmiths who make pneumatic picks should not harden them properly, so that they will quickly grow dull.

(3) You can easily put your pneumatic pick out of order. Pour a small amount of water through the oil lever and your pick will stop working. Coal dust and improper lubrication will also put it out of order.

(4) Weaken the chain that pulls the bucket conveyers carrying coal. A deep dent in the chain made with blows of a pick or shovel will cause it to part under normal strain. Once a chain breaks, normally or otherwise take your time about reporting the damage; be slow about taking the chain up for repairs and bringing it back down after repairs.

(5) Derail mine cars by putting obstructions on the rails and in switch points. If possible, pick a gallery where coal cars have to pass each other, so that traffic will be snarled up.

(6) Send up quantities of rock and other useless material with the coal.

(5) *Production: Agriculture*

(a) Machinery

(1) See par. 5 b. (2) (c), (d), (e).

(b) Crops and livestock probably will be destroyed only in areas where there are large food surpluses or where the enemy (regime) is known to be requisitioning food.

(1.) Feed crops to livestock. Let crops harvest too early or too late. Spoil stores of grain, fruit and vegetables by soaking them in water so that they will rot. Spoil fruit and vegetables by leaving them in the sun.

(6) *Transportation: Railways*

(a) Passengers

(1.) Make train travel as inconvenient as possible for enemy personnel. Make mistakes in issuing train tickets, leaving portions of the journey uncovered by the ticket book; issue two tickets for the same seat in the train, so that an interesting argument will result; near train time, instead of issuing printed tickets write them out slowly by hand, prolonging the process until the train is nearly ready to leave or has left the station. On station bulletin boards announcing train arrivals and departures, see that false and misleading information is given about trains bound for enemy destinations.

(2) In trains bound for enemy destinations, attendants should make life as uncomfortable as possible for passengers. See that the food is especially bad, take up tickets after midnight, call all station stops very loudly during the night, handle baggage as noisily as possible during the night, and so on.

(3) See that the luggage of enemy personnel is mislaid or unloaded at the wrong stations.

Switch address labels on enemy baggage.

(4) Engineers should see that trains run slow or make unscheduled stops for plausible reasons.

(b) Switches, Signals and Routing

(1) Exchange wires in switchboards containing signals and switches, so that they connect to the wrong terminals.

(2) Loosen push-rods so that signal arms do not work; break signal lights; exchange the colored lenses on red and green lights.

(3) Spread and spike switch points in the track so that they will not move, or place rocks or close-packed dirt between the switch points.

(4) Sprinkle rock salt or ordinary salt profusely over the electrical connections of switch points and on the ground nearby. When it rains, the switch will be short-circuited.

(5) See that cars are put on the wrong trains. Remove the labels from cars needing repair and put them on cars in good order. Leave couplings between cars as loose as possible.

(c) Road-beds and Open Track

(1) On a curve, take the bolts out of the tie-plates connecting to sections of the outside rail, and scoop away the gravel, cinders, or dirt for a few feet on each side of the connecting joint.

(2) If by disconnecting the tie-plate at a joint and loosening sleeper nails on each side of the joint, it becomes possible to move a sections of rail, spread two sections of rail and drive a spike vertically between them.

(d) Oil and Lubrication

(1) See 5 b. (2) (b).

(2) Squeeze lubricating pipes with pincers or dent them with hammers, so that the flow of oil is obstructed.

(e) Cooling Systems

(1) See 5 b (2) (c).

(f) Gasoline and Oil Fuel

(1) See 5 b (2) (d).

(g) Electric Motors

(1) See 5 b (2) (e) and (f).

(h) Boilers

(1) See 5 b (2) (h).

(2) After inspection put heavy oil or tar in the engines' boilers, or put half a kilogram of soft soap into the water in the tender.

(i) Brakes and Miscellaneous

(1) Engines should run at high speeds and use brakes excessively at curves and on downhill grades.

(2) Punch holes in air-brake valves or water supply pipes.

(3) In the last car of a passenger train or or a front car of a freight, remove the wadding from a journal box and replace it with oily rags.

(7) *Transportation: Automotive*

(a) Roads. Damage to roads [(3) below] is slow, and therefore impractical as a D-day or near D-day activity.

(1) Change sign posts at intersections and forks; the enemy will go the wrong way and it may be miles before he discovers his mistakes.

In areas where traffic is composed primarily of enemy autos, trucks, and motor convoys of various kinds remove danger signals from curves and intersections.

(2) When the enemy asks for directions, give him wrong information. Especially when enemy convoys are in the neighborhood, truck drivers can spread rumors and give false information about bridges being out, ferries closed, and detours lying ahead.

(3) If you can start damage to a heavily traveled road, passing traffic and the elements will do the rest. Construction gangs can see that too much sand or water is put in concrete or that the road foundation has soft spots. Anyone can scoop ruts in asphalt and macadam roads which turn soft in hot weather; passing trucks will accentuate the ruts to a point where substantial repair will be needed. Dirt roads also can be

scooped out. If you are a road laborer, it will be only a few minutes work to divert a small stream from a sluice so that it runs over and eats away the road.

(4) Distribute broken glass, nails, and sharp rocks on roads to puncture tires.

(b) Passengers

(1) Bus-driver can go past the stop where the enemy wants to get off. Taxi drivers can waste the enemy's time and make extra money by driving the longest possible route to his destination.

(c) Oil and Lubrication

(1) See 5 b. (2) (b).

(2) Disconnect the oil pump; this will burn out the main bearings in less than 50 miles of normal driving.

(d) Radiator

(1) See 5 b. (2) (c).

(e) Fuel

(1) See 5 b. (2) (d).

(f) Battery and Ignition

(1) Jam bits of wood into the ignition lock; loosen or exchange connections behind the switchboard; put dirt in spark plugs; damage distributor points.

(2) Turn on the lights in parked cars so that the battery will run down.

(3) Mechanics can ruin batteries in a number of undetectable ways: Take the valve cap off a cell, and drive a screw driver slantwise into the exposed water vent, shattering the plates of the cell; no damage will show when you put the cap back on. Iron or copper filings put into the cells i.e., dropped into the acid, will greatly shorten its life. Copper

coins or a few pieces of iron will accomplish the same and more slowly.

One hundred to 150 cubic centimeters of vinegar in each cell greatly reduces the life of the battery, but the odor of the vinegar may reveal what has happened.

(g) Gears

(1) Remove the lubricant from or put too light a lubricant in the transmission and other gears.

(2) In trucks, tractors, and other machines with heavy gears, fix the gear case insecurely, putting bolts in only half the bolt holes. The gears will be badly jolted in use and will soon need repairs.

(h) Tires

(1) Slash or puncture tires of unguarded vehicles. Put a nail inside a match box or other small box, and set it vertically in front of the back tire of a stationary car; when the car starts off, the nail will go neatly through the tire.

(2) It is easy to damage a tire in a tire repair shop: In fixing flats, spill glass, benzine, caustic soda, or other material inside the casing which will puncture or corrode the tube. If you put a gummy substance inside the tube, the next flat will stick the tube to the casing and make it unusable. Or, when you fix a flat tire, you can simply leave between the tube and the casing the object which caused the flat in the first place.

(3) In assembling a tire after repair, pump the tube up as fast as you can. Instead of filling out smoothly, it may crease, in which case it will wear out quickly. Or, as you put a tire together, see if you can pinch the tube between the rim of the tire and the rim of the wheel, so that a blow-out will result.

(4) In putting air into tires, see that they are kept below normal pressure, so that more than an ordinary amount of wear will result. In filling tires on double wheels, inflate the

inner tire to a much higher pressure than the outer one; both will wear out more quickly this way. Badly aligned wheels also wear tires out quickly; you can leave wheels out of alignment when they come in for adjustment, or you can spring them out of true with a strong kick, or by driving the car slowly and diagonally into a curb.

(5) If you have access to stocks of tires, you can rot them by spilling oil, gasoline, caustic acid, or benzine on them. Synthetic rubber, however, is less susceptible to these chemicals.

(8) *Transportation: Water*

(a) Navigation

(1) Barge and river boat personnel should spread false rumors about the navigability and conditions of the waterways they travel. Tell other barge and boat captains to follow channels that will take extra time, or cause them to make canal detours.

(2) Barge and river boat captains should navigate with exceeding caution near locks and bridges, to waste their time and to waste the time of other craft which may have to wait on them. If you don't pump the bilges of ships and barges often enough, they will be slower and harder to navigate. Barges "accidentally" run aground are an efficient time waster too.

(3) Attendants on swing, draw, or bascule bridges can delay traffic over the bridge or in the waterway underneath by being slow. Boat captains can leave unattended draw bridges open in order to hold up road traffic.

(4) Add or subtract compensating magnets to the compass on cargo ships. Demagnetize the compass or maladjust it by concealing a large bar of steel or iron near to it.

(b) Cargo

(1) While loading or unloading, handle cargo carelessly in order to cause damage. Arrange the cargo so that the weakest and lightest crates and boxes will be at the bottom of the hold, while the heaviest ones are on top of them.

Put hatch covers and tarpaulins on sloppily, so that rain and deck wash will injure the cargo.

Tie float valves open so that storage tanks will overflow on perishable goods.

(9) *Communications*

(a) Telephone

(1) At office, hotel and exchange switch boards delay putting enemy calls through, give them wrong numbers, cut them off "accidentally," or forget to disconnect them so that the line cannot be used again.

(2) Hamper official and especially military business by making at least one telephone call a day to an enemy headquarters; when you get them, tell them you have the wrong number.

Call military or police offices and make anonymous false reports of fires, air raids, bombs.

(3) In offices and buildings used by the enemy, unscrew the earphone of telephone receivers and remove the diaphragm. Electricians and telephone repair men can make poor connections and damage insulation so that cross talk and other kinds of electrical interference will make conversations hard or impossible to understand.

(4) Put the batteries under automatic switchboards out of commission by dropping nails, metal filings, or coins into the cells. If you can treat half the batteries in this way, the switchboard will stop working. A whole telephone system can be disrupted if you can put 10 percent of the cells in half the batteries of the central battery room out of order.

(b) Telegraph

(1) Delay the transmission and delivery of telegrams to enemy destinations.

(2) Garble telegrams to enemy destinations so that another telegram will have to be sent or a long distance call will have to be made. Sometimes it will be possible to do this by changing a single letter in a word—for example, changing "minimum" to "maximum," so that the person receiving the telegram will not know whether "minimum" or "maximum" is meant.

(c) Transportation Lines

(1) Cut telephone and telegraph transmission lines. Damage insulation on power lines to cause interference.

(d) Mail

(1) Post office employees can see to it that enemy mail is always delayed by one day or more, that it is put in wrong sacks, and so on.

(e) Motion Pictures

(1) Projector operators can ruin newsreels and other enemy propaganda films by bad focusing, speeding up or slowing down the film and by causing frequent breakage in the film.

(2) Audiences can ruin enemy propaganda films by applauding to drown the words of the speaker, by coughing loudly, and by talking.

(3) Anyone can break up a showing of an enemy propaganda film by putting two or three dozen large moths in a paper bag. Take the bag to the movies with you, put it on the floor in an empty section of the theater as you go in and leave it open. The moths will fly out and climb into the projector beam, so that the film will be obscured by fluttering shadows.

(f) Radio

(1) Station engineers will find it quite easy to overmodulate transmissions of talks by persons giving enemy propaganda or instructions, so that they will sound as if they were talking through a heavy cotton blanket with a mouth full of marbles.

(2) In your own apartment building, you can interfere with radio reception at times when the enemy wants everybody to listen. Take an electric light plug off the end of an electric light cord; take some wire out of the cord and tie it across two terminals of a two-prong plug or three terminals of a four-prong plug. Then take it around and put it into as many wall and floor outlets as you can find. Each time you insert the plug into a new circuit, you will blow out a fuse and silence all radios running on power from that circuit until a new fuse is put in.

(3) Damaging insulation on any electrical equipment tends to create radio interference in the immediate neighborhood, particularly on large generators, neon signs, fluorescent lighting, X-ray machines, and power lines. If workmen can damage insulation on a high tension line near an enemy airfield, they will make ground-to-plane radio communications difficult and perhaps impossible during long periods of the day.

(10) *Electric Power*

(a) Turbines, Electric Motors, Transformers

(1) See 5 b. (2) (e), (f),and (g).

(b) Transmission Lines

(1.) Linesmen can loosen and dirty insulators to cause power leakage. It will be quite easy, too, for them to tie a piece of very heavy string several times back and forth between two parallel transmission lines, winding it several turns around the wire each time. Beforehand, the string should be heavily saturated with salt and then dried. When it rains, the string becomes a conductor, and a short-circuit will result.

(11) *General Interference with Organizations and Production*

(a) Organizations and Conferences (1) Insist on doing everything through "channels." Never permit short-cuts to be taken in order to expedite decisions.

(2) Make "speeches." Talk as frequently as possible and at great length. Illustrate your "points" by long anecdotes and accounts of personal experiences. Never hesitate to make a few appropriate "patriotic" comments.

(3) When possible, refer all matters to committees, for "further study and consideration." Attempt to make the committees as large as possible—never less than five.

(4) Bring up irrelevant issues as frequently as possible.

(5) Haggle over precise wordings of communications, minutes, resolutions.

(6) Refer back to matters decided upon at the last meeting and attempt to re-open the question of the advisability of that decision.

(7) Advocate "caution." Be "reasonable" and urge your fellow-conferees to be "reasonable" and avoid haste which might result in embarrassments or difficulties later on.

(8) Be worried about the propriety of any decision—raise the question of whether such action as is contemplated lies within the jurisdiction of the group or whether it might conflict with the policy of some higher echelon.

(b) Managers and Supervisors

(1) Demand written orders.

(2) "Misunderstand" orders. Ask endless questions or engage in long correspondence about such orders. Quibble over them when you can.

(3) Do everything possible to delay the delivery of orders. Even though parts of an order may be ready beforehand, don't deliver it until it is completely ready.

(4) Don't order new working materials until your current stocks have been virtually exhausted, so that the slightest delay in filling your order will mean a shutdown.

(5) Order high-quality materials which are hard to get. If you don't get them argue about it. Warn that inferior materials will mean inferior work.

(6) In making work assignments, always sign out the unimportant jobs first. See that the important jobs are assigned to inefficient workers of poor machines.

(7) Insist on perfect work in relatively unimportant products; send back for refinishing those which have the least flaw. Approve other defective parts whose flaws are not visible to the naked eye.

(8) Make mistakes in routing so that parts and materials will be sent to the wrong place in the plant.

(9) When training new workers, give incomplete or misleading instructions.

(10) To lower morale and with it, production, be pleasant to inefficient workers; give them undeserved promotions. Discriminate against efficient workers; complain unjustly about their work.

(11) Hold conferences when there is more critical work to be done.

(12) Multiply paper work in plausible ways.

Start duplicate files.

(13) Multiply the procedures and clearances involved in issuing instructions, pay checks, and so on. See that three people have to approve everything where one would do.

(14) Apply all regulations to the last letter.

(c) Office Workers

(1) Make mistakes in quantities of material when you are copying orders. Confuse similar names. Use wrong addresses.

(2) Prolong correspondence with government bureaus.

(3) Misfile essential documents.

(4) In making carbon copies, make one too few, so that an extra copying job will have to be done.

(5) Tell important callers the boss is busy or talking on another telephone.

(6) Hold up mail until the next collection.

(7) Spread disturbing rumors that sound like inside dope.

(d) Employees

(1) *Work slowly*. Think out ways to increase the number of movements necessary on your job: use a light hammer instead of a heavy one, try to make a small wrench do when a big one is necessary, use little force where considerable force is needed, and so on.

(2) Contrive as many interruptions to your work as you can: when changing the material on which you are working, as you would on a lathe or punch, take needless time to do it. If you are cutting, shaping or doing other measured work, measure dimensions twice as often as you need to. When you go to the lavatory, spend a longer time there than is necessary.

Forget tools so that you will have to go back after them.

(3) Even if you understand the language, pretend not to understand instructions in a foreign tongue.

(4) Pretend that instructions are hard to understand, and ask to have them repeated more than once. Or pretend that you are particularly anxious to do your work, and pester the foreman with unnecessary questions.

(5) Do your work poorly and blame it on bad tools, machinery, or equipment. Complain that these things are preventing you from doing your job right.

(6) Never pass on your skill and experience to a new or less skillful worker.

(7) Snarl up administration in every possible way. Fill out forms illegibly so that they will have to be done over; make mistakes or omit requested information in forms.

(8) If possible, join or help organize a group for presenting employee problems to the management. See that the procedures adopted are as inconvenient as possible for the management, involving the presence of a large number of employees at each presentation, entailing more than one meeting for each grievance, bringing up problems which are largely imaginary, and so on.

(9) Misroute materials.

(10) Mix good parts with unusable scrap and rejected parts.

(12) *General Devices for Lowering Morale and Creating Confusion*

(a) Give lengthy and incomprehensible explanations when questioned.

(b) Report imaginary spies or danger to the Gestapo or police.

(c) Act stupid.

(d) Be as irritable and quarrelsome as possible without getting yourself into trouble.

(e) Misunderstand all sorts of regulations concerning such matters as rationing, transportation, traffic regulations.

(f) Complain against ersatz materials.

(g) In public treat axis nationals or quislings coldly.

(h) Stop all conversation when axis nationals or quislings enter a cafe.

(i) Cry and sob hysterically at every occasion, especially when confronted by government clerks.

(j) Boycott all movies, entertainments, concerts, newspapers which are in any way connected with the quisling authorities.

(k) Do not cooperate in salvage schemes.

www.ingramcontent.com/pod-product-compliance
Lightning Source LLC
LaVergne TN
LVHW051107180726
843512LV00020B/1647